PowerKids Readers:

MY SCHOOL™

Meet the Principal

Elizabeth Vogel

The Rosen Publishing Group's
PowerKids Press™
New York

1

Rosen Publishing would like to extend special thanks to Superintendent Robert Watson, Darlene Davis, and the children in Ms. Dixon's class of the City of Poughkeepsie S.F.B. Morse Young Child Magnet School.

Published in 2002 by The Rosen Publishing Group, Inc.
29 East 21st Street, New York, NY 10010

First Edition

Book Design: Michael Donnellan

Photo Credits: All photos by Cindy Reiman.

Vogel, Elizabeth.
Meet the principal / Elizabeth Vogel.— 1st ed.
    p. cm. — (My school)
Includes bibliographical references (p.   ) and index.
  ISBN 0-8239-6033-1 (lib. bdg.)
1. School principals—Juvenile literature. [1. School principals. 2. Occupations.]
I. Title.
  LB2831.9 .V64 2002
  371.2'012—dc21

                                                    2001000952

Manufactured in the United States of America

Contents

I am the school principal.
I work with the students,
parents, and teachers.

You can usually find me in my office, but I also like to visit your classroom.

Sometimes I say hello to you in the hall.

I help students learn the school rules. Some school rules are to listen to your teacher, to be kind to your fellow students, and not to talk during a class lesson.

Our School Expectations:
1. Listen to your teacher.
2. Be kind to your fellow students.
3. No talking during a class lesson.

Sometimes you come to talk to me.

I am also in charge of making sure the teachers are happy with the school. They might need more pens and paper. We also talk about ways to make the school even better.

15

Sometimes I work in my office. Principals have a lot of work to do.

I like to see you on the playground, too. School is a great place to learn and play.

I am in charge of the whole school. I make sure the school day goes smoothly.

Words to Know

principal's office

paper

pen

playground

Here is another book to read about principals:

School Principals (Community Helpers)
by Tracey Borass and Sidney Morrison
Bridgestone Books

To learn more about principals, check out this Web site:

http://home.nycap.rr.com/cjem/ems/
 page4.html

Index

Word Count: 157

Note to Librarians, Teachers, and Parents

PowerKids Readers are specially designed to help emergent and beginning readers build their skills in reading for information. Simple vocabulary and concepts are paired with stunning, detailed images from the natural world around them. Readers will respond to written language by linking meaning with their own everyday experiences and observations. Sentences are short and simple, employing a basic vocabulary of sight words, as well as new words that describe objects or processes that take place in the natural world. Large type, clean design, and photographs corresponding directly to the text all help children to decipher meaning. Features such as a contents page, picture glossary, and index help children get the most out of PowerKids Readers. They also introduce children to the basic elements of a book, which they will encounter in their future reading experiences. Lists of related books and Web sites encourage kids to explore other sources and to continue the process of learning.